Torah: The Fountainhead of Wisdom

Walking in the Way of Christ & the Apostles
Study Guide Series
Part 1, Book 5
A 7-Session Study

Peter Briggs

ISBN: 9781947642058

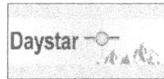

Daystar

Published by:
Daystar Institute / NM, Inc.
P.O. Box 50567
Albuquerque, NM 87181
www.DaystarInstituteNM.us

Distributed in Africa by:
Daystar Institute / Africa
Kampala, Uganda
www.DaystarInstituteAfrica.org

Table of Contents

List of Figures

WitW
Walking in the Way of
Christ & the Apostles

Foreword

Jesus Christ, in His three-year ministry with His twelve disciples, modeled the method for teaching disciples to walk in His way.

The Walking in the Way (WitW) Study Guide Series attempts to model Christ's method of teaching by utilizing a holistic approach designed to challenge students to apply biblical principles to their lives and ministries. Our aim is to equip disciples of Jesus to "walk in him, rooted and built up in him and established in the faith, just as you were taught, abounding in thanksgiving." Colossians 2:6,7. Thus, we emphasize wholehearted discipleship, practical Christian theology, and a biblical world view.

We have prayerfully designed the WitW study materials to equip you with the tools and concepts needed to achieve this goal. May the word of God dwell in our hearts richly through faith by studying it, reflecting upon it, and allowing it to penetrate the deepest recesses of our souls. By this means, we bring our hearts and minds into alignment with God's heart and mind.

How to Use this Study Guide

Although this Bible study may be done independently, we strongly recommend using it in a group setting. Study each session prayerfully and reflect deeply on the included passages of Scripture as part of your daily devotional time with God. Establish a journal in which you record your answers to questions, as well as your reflections and notes.

If you are participating in a group study, be prepared to interact with your leader and group members. This includes sharing insights and practical lessons God is teaching you personally. Read the questions and associated Scripture passages aloud and stick to the Bible as your sole authority for answers given. At the end of each discussion session, take time to pray for group member needs; then hold one another accountable for putting the lessons learned into practice.

Upon completion of one book, move on to the next book in the series. In parallel, begin sharing the WitW teaching with family members, work associates, and others in your circle of influence.

Leaders may use their discretion as to how much material to cover in any given discussion session. We also encourage Bible study teachers and leaders to read the associated WitW Theological Handbook or Theological Reader in order to gain a better understanding of the material presented in this booklet. Our resources are listed in the back of this study guide and are available on Amazon.com.

Introduction to Book 5

The Torah (Hebrew for instruction) is comprised of the first five books of the Hebrew Scriptures: Genesis, Exodus, Leviticus, Numbers, and Deuteronomy. In these books of Moses, we learn about the origin of the earth and its inhabitants, God's purpose in creation, the introduction of sin and its consequences, and God's redemptive plan to ultimately restore man and the planet. Its scope covers all of time as we know it. In these five books are found the answers to man's fundamental questions about life and purpose. For these reasons we call it the fountainhead of wisdom.

In this study guide we will identify and explore a number of motifs or themes which find their inception in Torah and are developed throughout the Hebrew and Christian Scriptures.

Book 5 Goals

To appreciate the Torah as the fountainhead of wisdom in which all the major motifs or themes of the Bible are introduced.

To recognize and appreciate the significance of each of the fourteen integrative motifs.

To learn how to trace a motif from its introduction in the Torah, through its development in the Hebrew Scriptures, through the Christ Event, and to its culmination in the Christian Scriptures.

Session 1. Torah: The Fountainhead of Wisdom – Part One

Overview

In this study guide, we will focus on the primary importance of the Torah, the first five books of the Bible. It is in these initial books of the Bible that all the themes or motifs of the Bible are introduced. These motifs are then developed in the Hebrew Scriptures (or Old Testament), actualized in the person of Jesus Christ and culminated at Christ's return.

Thus, it is entirely appropriate for us to designate the Torah as the fountainhead of wisdom.

We have identified fourteen integrative motifs that originate in the Torah. Five of these are developed in TR1; they are identified below in bold. Two of the motifs are unpacked in this study guide.

Integrative Motifs Introduced in the Torah

1.   The Name of God
2.   The Temple
3.   The Sabbath
4.   The Imago Dei
5.   The Marriage Metaphor
6.   The Invasion of Evil, Sin, and Death
7.   The Seed of the Woman
8.   The Acceptable Sacrifice
9.   The City of Man vs. the Kingdom of God
10.   The People of the New Way
11.   The Gospel
12.   Sovereign Election and Human Responsibility
13.   The Prototype
14.   The Covenant of Conditional Blessing

Figure 1 illustrates the progression of a motif from its inception in the Torah through its development in the Hebrew Scriptures to its actualization in the person of Christ, to its culmination at Christ's return.

1. Progressive Development of Integrative Motifs

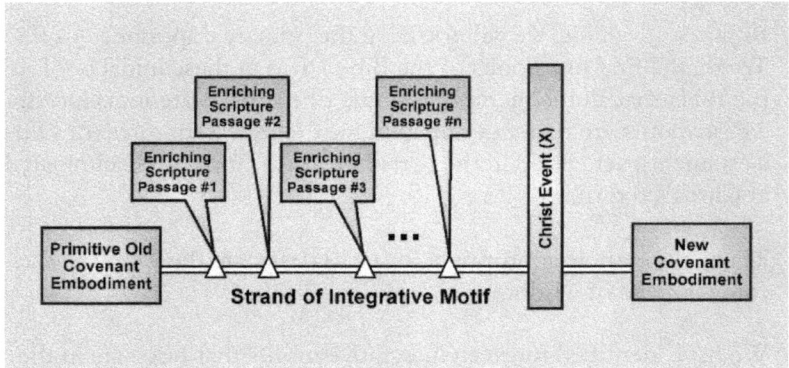

Keep this figure in mind as you become briefly acquainted with each of the motifs in the overview which follows. Also ponder the significance of each motif in God's eternal plan.

Motif #1. The Name of God

We speak of the divine name in the singular because that is the way in which the biblical authors always refer to it.

The name of God embodies all that He is in His nature and character.

However, because of God's manifold nature and character and the infinite dimensionality of His Person, the Hebrew Scriptures employ a multitude of divine names, a number of which are compound names. Each of these reveals an important facet of God's nature and character.

The following two verses from the 1st and 2nd chapters of Genesis introduce the two most important names of God.

> **Genesis 1:1.** In the beginning God created the heavens and the earth.

> **Genesis 2:4.** These are the records of the heavens and the earth, concerning their creation at the time that the Lord God made the earth and the heavens.

The manner in which the divine names have been translated from the Hebrew Scriptures into English has tended to blur their distinctive meanings. Therefore, through the WitW study we will endeavor to acquire an appreciation for the Hebraic names of God.

Elohim, the Absolutely Transcendent God

The divine name employed throughout the 1st chapter of Genesis beginning with the 1st verse is Elohim, and it is translated as "God" in our English Bibles. This is the plural of El, which is the generic divine name in the Canaanite language.

Q 1.   Why do you suppose that the Holy Spirit prompted Moses to employ the plural form of El in Genesis 1:1? What is the significance of the plural?

You may have suggested that Elohim is a primitive reflection of the three Persons of the Trinity – God the Father, God the Son, and God the Spirit. While I regard this answer as reasonable, it may not be the principal reason why the Holy Spirit prompted Moses to employ the plural of El.

That principal reason was probably to impart the sense of absolute transcendence, which means that God is absolutely separate from and infinitely higher than His creation.

Beginning with the 4th verse of the 2nd chapter of Genesis, we encounter the compound name Yahweh Elohim, which is rendered "Lord God" in most of our modern English Bibles. God's proper or personal name appears as YHWH in Hebrew, which is termed the Tetragrammaton by theologians. In biblical Hebrew, the vowel sounds are defined by points or special marks associated with the consonants. We pronounce God's personal name as Yahweh.

With this understood, we can now point out that Elohim is not a personal name, but rather an appellative name or title like "doctor."

Q 2.   Why do you suppose the Holy Spirit prompted Moses to employ Yahweh Elohim in the narrative of the 2nd chapter of Genesis? What is the significance of combining God's personal name with His title in the compound name Yahweh Elohim?

If your answer to this question was to impart a sense of relational nearness, I believe you are correct. Whereas Elohim imparts the sense of absolute transcendence, Yahweh imparts the sense of absolute nearness or immanence.

In the narrative of the 1st chapter, God's absolute transcendence is emphasized, and in the narrative of the 2nd chapter, His absolute immanence and relational nearness is emphasized as well.

The opening verses of the 91st Psalm allow me to introduce two other important names of God.

Psalm 91:1-2

The one who lives under the protection of the Most High dwells in the shadow of the Almighty.

I will say to the Lord, "My refuge and my fortress, my God, in whom I trust."

Allow me now to insert the Hebraic divine names instead of the English words that are used to translate them in this passage.

The one who lives under the protection of El Elyon dwells in the shadow of El Shaddai.

I will say to Yahweh, "My refuge and my fortress, my Elohim, in whom I trust."

The divine name, El Shaddai is most interesting and significant. Shad is the Hebrew word for "breast," so El Shaddai imparts the sense of "the great breasted One." It imparts the sense that God is able to nurture and comfort His children.

Q 3.   With this understood, analyze the flow of thought in Psalm 91:1-2 with regard to the unfolding of the nature and character of God and our relationship to Him.

Read Genesis 14:17-20, Genesis 16:13-16, Genesis 22:14, Exodus 15:25-26, Exodus 17:15-16, Exodus 31:12-17, Psalm 23:1, Jeremiah 23:5-6, and Ezekiel 48:35.

Q 4.   Each of the passages listed above reveals a compound name of God. Try to identify the divine name revealed by each passage together with the theological significance of that name. Briefly summarize the setting in which each name was revealed, including the person or persons to whom it was revealed.

Genesis 14:17-20 / El Roi / The God who sees me

Genesis 16:13-16 / El Elyon / God Most High

Genesis 22:14 / Yahweh Jireh / Yahweh who provides

Exodus 15:25-26 / Yahweh Rophe / Yahweh who heals

Exodus 17:15-16 / Yahweh Nissi / Yahweh our banner

Exodus 31:12-17 / Yahweh M'Qadash / Yahweh who sanctifies

Psalm 23:1 / Yahweh Rohi / Yahweh our shepherd

Jeremiah 23:5-6 / Yahweh Tsidkenu / Yahweh our righteousness

Ezekiel 48:35 / Yahweh Shammah / Yahweh is there

From this point onward, the divine names will not be italicized; this is to signify the fact that we are endeavoring to incorporate them into our vocabulary to facilitate our appreciating the nature and character of God.

Motif #2. The Temple

The temple is that place or sphere in which man can approach, worship, and enjoy fellowship with God.

Read Genesis 1:26-28 and Genesis 2:8.

Q 5.   Where was the first temple and what was its significance?

Indeed, the primordial temple was the Garden of Eden. There God declared that the man whom He had created was to be fruitful and multiply so as to fill the entire earth, and he was to have dominion over the entire terrestrial creation. We believe this is a reflection of the fact that God intended from the beginning that His temple would encompass the entire earth, and that all peoples would worship Him and have access to fellowship with Him.

The post-Fall temple is the Tabernacle in the Wilderness and presents the first comprehensive biblical representation of the means by which fallen man could approach, worship, and enjoy fellowship with Yahweh, the absolutely holy God of Israel. The Tabernacle in the Wilderness is depicted in Figure 4 of Book 3, and it is discussed in Session 5 of that book.

Motif #3. The Sabbath

Yahweh set apart one day in seven for rest, reflection upon and worship of Yahweh, and fellowship with one another.

Read Genesis 2:1-3 and Exodus 31:12-17.

Q 6.   When did the Sabbath first originate, and what is its purpose?

As you probably stated in response to the question above, God blessed and consecrated the Sabbath as one day in seven in which man should rest from his labors, devote himself to reflection upon God and His ways, worship God, and enjoy fellowship with one another. In the Exodus passage, God declares Himself to be

11

Yahweh M'Qadash – the God who makes us holy – in connection with the faithful keeping of the Sabbath on the part of His people.

In Exodus 31:12-17 Sabbath-keeping is linked to the process of sanctification. The weekly Sabbath is a microcosm of our eternal Sabbath, which will be devoted entirely to reflection upon and worship of Yahweh and fellowship with one another.

Motif #4. The Imago Dei

Imago Dei is the Latin phrase which means the image of God.

Read Genesis 1:26-28 and Genesis 2:7.

Q 7.   What does being made in the image of God mean to you?

According to Genesis 1:26-28, Yahweh created man in His own image and according to His likeness. According to Genesis 2:7, He accomplished this by conjoining two substances, one material and the other immaterial: namely, a body formed from "the dust from the ground," and "the breath of life," which is a reference to the human spirit.

The conjoining of the human body with the human spirit brought into being something altogether new; namely, a human soul.

Motif #5. The Marriage Metaphor

The principal purpose of human marriage is to serve as a metaphor for the relationship between Christ and His church.

Read Genesis 2:18-25 and Ephesians 5:22-33.

Q 8.   How do these passages represent the relationship between a man and a woman in human marriage?

According to Genesis 2:18-25, human marriage was instituted by God Himself. With the unfolding revelation in the Hebrew Scriptures, the fact becomes evident that human marriage serves as a metaphor of God's relationship with His people.

The three divinely ordained purposes of human marriage are as follows:

> To represent God's covenant relationship with His people.

> For the procreation and raising up of godly children.

> For human enjoyment.

Human marriage and the Christian household is one of the ways which God has ordained that human societies would be ordered to mediate His kingly authority to the world of mankind. This concept is developed in Book 11 of WitW Part 2.

Motif #6. The Invasion of Evil, Sin, and Death

The serpent beguiled Eve to taste of the forbidden fruit and then to convince her husband to rebel against Yahweh's explicit prohibition and eat as well. By this means, Satan

caused evil, sin, and death to invade the terrestrial domain
that had been placed under Adam's rule.

Sessions 3 and 4 of this study guide are devoted to an in-depth discussion of this motif. Also, it is the first of five that are discussed in detail in chapter 5 of TR1; I encourage you to refer to this discussion to further deepen and enrich your understanding.

Motif #7. The Seed of the Woman

Embedded in the curse that Yahweh Elohim pronounced against the serpent was the promise that a man would come forth from the seed of the woman, and he would conquer the serpent.

Genesis 3:15. I will put hostility between you and the woman, and between your seed and her seed. He will strike your head, and you will strike his heel.

Q 9. Formulate a paraphrase of this verse using words that are both familiar to you and which are also true to the author's intended meaning. Discuss the significance of this verse.

After announcing The Seed of the Woman in Genesis 3:15, the Genesis narrative traces this mysterious strand of DNA through the patriarchal genealogies to Abraham. In Genesis 15:5, God promises to give Abraham a great multitude of offspring or seed. In fact, the Hebrew word translated offspring in this verse is zera, the same word translated "seed" in Genesis 3:15. In Galatians 3:16, Paul identifies the singular Descendant of Abraham through whom this promise is fulfilled – namely, Yeshua Ha Mashiach or Jesus the Messiah. It is noteworthy that God's promise of descendants to Abraham was the particular focus of Abraham's faith response, on which basis God imputed righteousness to him according to Genesis 15:6.

Notes and Reflections

Session 2. Torah, the Fountainhead of Wisdom – Part Two

Motif #8. The Acceptable Sacrifice

The bloody sacrifice involving the death of an innocent substitute was pioneered by Yahweh Elohim Himself in providing garments to cover the nakedness of Adam and Eve after the Fall.

> **Genesis 3:21.** Yahweh Elohim made clothing out of skins for Adam and his wife, and He clothed them. [Adapted from the HCSB]

Q 1.   Discuss the symbolism of Yahweh Elohim's slaughtering of innocent animals to provide durable clothing for Adam and Eve.

According to the verse above, Yahweh Elohim replaced the garments of fig leaves that Adam and Eve had fabricated for themselves with garments of animal skins. By this act, Yahweh Elohim initiated a sacrificial trajectory that runs through the entire Scripture. To provide those skins, animals were slaughtered by the hand of Yahweh Elohim Himself. Because man's sin is a capital offense against an absolutely holy and righteous God, it is only through the shedding of the blood of an innocent substitute that a covering for sin can be provided.

Motif #9. The City of Man Versus the Kingdom of God

The apex of mankind's prideful rebellion against Yahweh Elohim is the Tower of Babel episode recorded in the 11th chapter of Genesis. It is noteworthy that the Hebrew word that is translated as "Babylon" in the HCSB rendering of Genesis 11:9 is identical to that which designates the ancient city of Babylon later in the Hebrew Scriptures. The traditional name of the city in Genesis 11:9 according to most English translations is "Babel," which blurs the correspondence between this city and the ancient city of Babylon. Thus, we would be entirely correct to rename the episode recorded in the 11th chapter of Genesis as the Tower of Babylon episode. In fact, I will use this terminology going forward.

Accordingly, the ancient city of Babylon introduced in the 11th chapter of Genesis is the paradigmatic city of man. Babylon embodies and represents the prideful rebellion of mankind against the righteous rule of Yahweh Elohim, which is expressed by our obsession to be god without God.

Read Genesis 11 and Revelation 17.

Q 2.   Identify and discuss the significance of the common factor that is present in both of these chapters.

Q 3.   With the correspondence between the Tower of Babylon episode recorded in the 11th chapter of Genesis and the ancient city of Babylon now understood, identify and list the points of conflict between Babylon as the paradigmatic city of man and the kingdom of God, including the biblical passage where each conflict is recorded.

Motif #10. People of the New Way

This integrative motif is the second of five that are discussed in detail in chapter 5 of TR1.

With the apex of mankind's prideful rebellion against the righteous rule of Yahweh recorded in the 11th chapter of Genesis, the literary turn that we experience as we consider the calling of Abraham in the 12th chapter could hardly be more dramatic.

Yahweh abandons His dealings with mankind as a whole when He calls out and sets apart a single family – that of Abraham – through whom He would begin to mediate His kingly rule to the rest of Adam's race.

Yahweh called out and set apart Abraham as the pioneer and progenitor of a new way. In Genesis 18:19 this new way is represented for the first time in Scripture as the "way of Yahweh."

Q 4.   How did the people of the new way differ from those of the old way?

Motif #11. The Gospel

This integrative motif is the third of five that are discussed in detail in chapter 5 of TR1. The motifs of The Seed of the Woman, The Acceptable Sacrifice, and The Gospel are tightly coupled, with all three originating in a single passage of Scripture, Genesis 3:14-21.

Embedded in the curse that Yahweh Elohim pronounced against the serpent was the promise that a Redeemer would come from the seed of the woman.

> **Genesis 3:15.** I will put hostility between you and the woman, and between your seed and her seed. He will strike your head, and you will strike his heel.

This important verse is designated the ***protoevangelium***; it is the very first announcement of the gospel in Scripture. It is then expanded in Yahweh's covenant with Abraham that he would be blessed in order to become a blessing to all nations and peoples. It would be through Abraham that the promised seed of the woman would ultimately emerge. Through that promised seed, the head of the serpent would be crushed, and all the effects of the invasion of evil, sin, and death would be obliterated.

> **Genesis 4:1.** Adam was intimate with his wife Eve, and she conceived and gave birth to Cain. She said, "I have had a male child with Yahweh's help." [Adapted from the HCSB]

Q 5.   Analyze Eve's statement after having given birth to Cain in relation to Genesis 3:15.

The unfolding narrative of the Hebrew Scriptures reveals a progression in the prophetic information regarding the promised Redeemer, and a corresponding progression in the Jew's anticipation of the promised Messiah or Anointed One. Eve's exclamation recorded in Genesis 4:1 suggests that she thought that her firstborn son was the one Yahweh had in mind in His Genesis 3:15 pronouncement.

18

Motif #12. Sovereign Election and Human Responsibility

The Genesis narrative reveals God's unconditional choice of a people for His kingdom apart from any human merit while at the same time holding people accountable for their self-determined choices.

An interesting pattern that we observe throughout the Book of Genesis is Yahweh's choosing the younger instead of the older to be the bearer of the covenant.

Abel and then Seth are chosen instead of Cain.

Isaac is chosen instead of Ishmael; Jacob is chosen instead of Esau; Judah and Joseph are chosen instead of Reuben. When Jacob blessed the two sons of Joseph, he elevated Ephraim, the younger, above his older brother, Manasseh.

Continuing into the Book of Exodus, Moses is chosen to be the deliverer of Israel instead of his older brother, Aaron. And the people of Israel are chosen to be God's special people instead of any of the other nations of the world. And then much later in biblical history, David is chosen instead of his older brothers to be king of Israel and the progenitor of the Messiah. Thus, through the narrative of the Hebrew Scriptures, God is making abundantly clear the fact that His choice is based upon parameters that only He can see, and it is not at all based upon anything for which we, the chosen ones, can take credit.

Q 6.   Would you consider God's choices of the men mentioned above as counter-cultural and is that typical of the manner in which God works? Explain your answer.

Intertwined with the theme of sovereign election, the Bible makes clear that self-determined human choices are important, and that God holds us accountable for making wise choices. This is clearly the case with Adam, who was given a single prohibition. As a result of his disobedience, the curse of evil, sin, and death fell upon him and all of us as his descendants.

Q 7.   How is Adam's choice an example of how God holds man accountable and responsible for his individual choices?

If you would like to dig deeper into the subject of sovereign election and human responsibility, I encourage you to study the section bearing this title in chapter 5 of TR1 and Appendix F in TR4.

Motif #13. The Prototype

Through the Exodus and Conquest episodes, the nation of Israel serves as a type or model of the individual disciple's experience of redemption and sanctification.

In their experience of the Exodus, desert wanderings, and Conquest episodes, the nation of Israel became a model, or prototype, of the individual new covenant believer. In particular, note the following parallels between Israel's experiences and a believer's maturing in his faith. We call this process sanctification.

The ten plagues in Egypt correspond to the experience of conviction of the bondage to evil, sin, and death and the desperate need for divine deliverance in the life of the individual whom God is drawing toward Christ.

The Passover in Egypt corresponds to the exercise of faith in the covering blood of Jesus Christ on the part of the individual disciple of Christ. In fact, John 1:29 relates the Passover lamb that was slain to "the Lamb of God, who takes away the sin of the world."

The Exodus from Egypt corresponds to the experience of redemption by the disciple of Christ on account of the atoning work of Jesus Christ.

The crossing of the Red Sea, also known as the Sea of Reeds, corresponds to the experience of water baptism by the disciple of Christ, which, in turn, serves as an outward representation of positional sanctification wrought by the Holy Spirit. Positional sanctification means that the disciple is declared to be holy and consecrated unto God on the basis of his faith in the atoning sacrifice of Jesus Christ.

The Conquest of the promised land corresponds to the experiential sanctification by means of which our positional state of being declared holy and consecrated unto God becomes progressively realized in our experience.

The tolerance of the residual Canaanites in the land corresponds to a failure to carry sanctification to completion by fully participating in the death of Jesus Christ, by means of which the flesh is made subject to the death of Christ, and thereby its power is neutralized.

Q 8.   Discuss the ways in which these pictures embedded into the experience of Israel as recorded in the Torah enrich and deepen your understanding of God's deliverance of us from bondage to evil, sin, and death.

Motif #14. The Covenant of Conditional Blessing

God has promised to bless those who fear Him, love Him, and walk in His way, and He has promised to curse those who refuse to do so.

The covenant that Yahweh enacted with the nation of Israel at Mt. Sinai followed the pattern of an ancient Hittite suzerain-vassal treaty. Such a treaty had three main components as follows:

> The laws that the vassal was to faithfully keep.

> The blessings of protection and prosperity that the suzerain would confer upon the vassal, so long as they adhered to the terms of the covenant.

> The cursings and punishments that would result from the vassal failing to keep the terms of the covenant.

All three of these components are present in the covenant of Mt. Sinai with Yahweh being the suzerain and the nation of Israel being His vassal. Regrettably, Israel broke that covenant, which resulted in their ultimate banishment from the land of promise.

However, as the story of the Hebrew Scriptures approaches its logical and theological conclusion, a remnant of Israel is restored to the land. According to the 8th and 9th chapters of Nehemiah, the people of Israel experienced glorious renewal and revival after the temple had been reconstructed, worship of Yahweh resumed, and the walls and gates of Jerusalem had been restored. This fulfilled the promise announced through Moses in the concluding chapters of Deuteronomy and confirmed to Solomon in 2 Chronicles 7:14.

There is a phrase that perfectly characterizes the overall trajectory of the Hebrew Scriptures: tears and fire, referring to our tears of contrition over sin, and the fire of the outpouring of the Spirit of God to bring about renewal and revival.

To dig deeper into the covenant of conditional blessing, I encourage you to read the section bearing this title in chapter 5 of TR1.

Summary

An awareness of the major motifs of the Bible enhances our understanding of Scripture as we read our Bibles both devotionally and for study. Spend some time reflecting on the fourteen motifs. Challenge yourself to think about how masterfully they are developed in Scripture, placing in evidence the dual authorship of Scripture; namely, the Holy Spirit and some forty human authors. Only God could superintend the weaving together of these themes throughout the Bible. Also, challenge yourself to reflect on the meaning of each of these themes and the practical lessons they contain that can be applied to your life and ministry.

Notes and Reflections

Session 3. The Invasion of Evil, Sin, and Death – Part One

In an effort to help you understand the progressive development of the integrative motifs in accordance with Figure 1, I have selected two that have important theological content as illustrations. While the first is dark and seemingly hopeless, the second is full of light and glory.

The first is Motif #6, upon which we touched in Session 1.

A Perfect Creation Marred by Evil, Sin, and Death

Read Genesis 1 & 2.

Q 1.   How does God represent His creation in Genesis 1:31?

God considered the creation of the cosmos, and most especially mankind, as very good. God was indeed pleased with His creation.

Read Genesis 3.

Q 2.   What changed in God's perfect creation?

It would certainly appear as though the serpent's beguilement of Adam and Eve to be like God and their subsequent sin of eating the forbidden fruit would qualify as an invasion of the enemy in an extremely successful frontal attack. This was indeed an invasion, but was it the first invasion of evil, sin, and death?

The Fall of Lucifer

Sometime prior to the scene portrayed in the 3rd chapter of Genesis, a cataclysmic confrontation occurred in heaven between God and one of his archangels.

Read Isaiah 14:12-24; Ezekiel 28:11-19.

Q 3.   Identify the names by which Lucifer is called in these two passages. Are these names to be taken literally or symbolically?

Both of these passages are allegorical in the sense that the author uses the kings of Babylon and Tyre to represent Lucifer.

Q 4.   List everything you learn concerning Lucifer from these two passages.

Take into account the following points.

> Lucifer was one of three archangels created by God. Isaiah 14:12 refers to the person in this passage as "shining morning star." The proper name "Lucifer," which literally means "morning star," is derived from this phrase. He was one of three archangels created by Yahweh Elohim, the other two being Gabriel and Michael.

> Lucifer was created perfect and beautiful in accordance with Ezekiel 28:12b-13.

Lucifer was the highest ranking archangel. Ezekiel 28:14 calls Lucifer "an anointed guardian cherub," the implication being that Lucifer was one of a number of similar angels. However, the implication of the Hebrew is that he was the singular anointed guardian cherub. Evidently, his office was to guard the very throne of Yahweh Elohim. As such, he was the highest ranking archangel, the crown jewel of the angelic creation.

Lucifer's fall was the result of prideful rebellion. Isaiah 14:13-14 and Ezekiel 28:15-17a both describe Lucifer's prideful rebellion.

Lucifer was expelled from his office and banished along with his entourage. Isaiah 14:15ff and Ezekiel 28:16ff recount Lucifer's eviction and his being cast down on account of his prideful rebellion.

Read Revelation 12:7ff.

In this passage the Apostle John uses highly figurative language to describe Lucifer's rebellion and expulsion from heaven.

Q 5.   How does John refer to Lucifer in this passage?

Lucifer is no longer known as the Morning Star, or the Son of the Dawn, but as Satan and the Devil.

Q 6.   What was the outcome of Satan's rebellion against Yahweh?

By means of his prideful rebellion against the righteous rule of Yahweh Elohim, Lucifer literally brought evil, sin, and death into being, where these had previously been absent from a perfect creation.

Having the power to freely choose between submission to the sovereign authority of Yahweh Elohim and rebellion, Lucifer chose the latter. This choice arose from the prideful assertion of his heart as stated in Isaiah 14:14, "I will make myself like the Most High." Choices matter!

While it is true that Yahweh Elohim allowed the possibility of evil, sin, and death by creating angels and mankind with free moral agency, Lucifer was the one who actualized evil in the cosmos by his own self-determined choice.

I submit that prideful rebellion against the sovereign rule of Yahweh Elohim lies at the heart of all evil and sin.

Q 7.   Analyze the statement above. Do you agree or disagree with it? Explain your answer.

The Fall of Man

Read Genesis 1:26-27.

Q 8.   What is the significance of man's being created in the image and likeness of God?

Among other things such as the capacity to think and reason, man was given the power of free moral agency, the capacity to know and choose between right and wrong. (Read Appendix F of TR4 for a careful analysis of the meaning of human free agency.)

Reread Genesis 2.

Q 9.   What was the relationship between man and Yahweh Elohim as recorded in the 2nd chapter of Genesis? What benefits accrued to man from that relationship?

Because of man's being in the divine image and likeness, he had the capacity for fellowship with Yahweh Elohim. In addition, he was assigned the role of regent over the terrestrial creation. Adam enjoyed an open and direct relationship with Yahweh Elohim, Eve, his wife, and all the animals.

Q 10.   What is the implication of man's having been created with free moral agency? Analyze why a cosmos in which free moral agency exists is superior to one in which it doesn't exist.

Because of the moral free agency with which man was created, and because of his regency over the earth, his moral choice had the potential of impacting the entire material cosmos. By definition however, only one sovereign will, God's, would determine what is good and evil, and that right was reserved to and exercised by Yahweh Elohim throughout the creative process. This exercise of moral authority by Yahweh Elohim culminated in the pronouncement of Genesis 1:31 that everything "was very good."

Q 11.   How does God's being the final moral authority in the cosmos relate to His having created man with free moral agency?

Reread Genesis 3.

The invasion of evil, sin, and death into the a previously perfect terrestrial sphere occurred when Lucifer, now Satan and the Devil, entered the Garden of Eden in the form of a talking serpent.

Q 12.   In Genesis 3:5 the serpent asserts, "For God knows that when you eat of it your eyes will be opened, and you will be like God, knowing good and evil." What is the implication of this assertion?

Satan, in effect, was offering Eve the ability to possess moral authority over determining good and evil. As a result, she ate the forbidden fruit and presented some to her husband.

Q 13.   What was the implication of Adam's response to his wife's choice to eat the forbidden fruit?

At this critical juncture, Adam was confronted with a dilemma. According to his understanding, if he refused to eat, then Eve would die, and he would be left alone. If he did eat, then they would both die together. What he failed to appreciate was a principle which became codified many centuries later in Numbers 30:3ff; that is, he could have nullified his wife's decision to eat of the forbidden fruit. I am convinced that Adam knew this in his unsullied human conscience, for, as an immutable divine principle in

> **1 Corinthians 10:1.** God is faithful, and He will not let you be tempted beyond what you are able, but with the temptation He will also provide a way of escape, that you are able to bear it.

Tragically, Adam failed to recognize and avail himself of the "way of escape," and he ate of the fruit offered to him by his wife.

As a result of his eating, not hers, we are told in Genesis 3:7:

Then the eyes of both of them were opened, and they knew that they were naked; so they sewed fig leaves together and made loincloths for themselves.

By his act of eating, Adam joined Eve's act of prideful rebellion and made it his own. As a couple, they chose to usurp the position that Yahweh Elohim had reserved unto Himself; that is, the moral authority to discern, and thereby to sovereignly determine, good and evil.

Q 14.   What was Adam's and Eve's first moral judgment?

The effect was immediate, as may be seen in Genesis 3:7-11. In particular, according to the 7th verse, Adam and Eve made their first moral judgment in the observation that they were naked, and that this was not good. Underlying their observation was the awareness of guilt resulting from their prideful rebellion against the singular commandment of Yahweh Elohim. The consequence was a schism between the two of them and an attempt to hide from Yahweh Elohim.

Read Romans 5:12-21.

Q 15.   How did Adam's act of disobedience impact the human race?

According to the Apostle Paul's divinely inspired analysis, when Adam ate, we all ate with him. As federal head, he was progenitor and representative of the entire human race before God.

Therefore, we all sinned at a point in time when Adam sinned. We all partook of his prideful rebellion, and we have been in rebellion against the righteous rule of God ever since, both by nature and by choice.

Read Genesis 2:15-18.

Q 16.   In the 17th verse, Yahweh Elohim states, "On the day you eat from it, you will certainly die." What is the implication of this statement?

Would Yahweh Elohim actually punish Adam and Eve by death for their treasonous act? No, but instead He slaughtered animals and provided blood-stained coverings for their naked bodies. By this means, He vividly displayed that the only way into renewed fellowship with Him required the death of an innocent substitute. While Adam's and Eve's attention was riveted upon the lifeless animal carcasses lying on the ground before them, God's eye was upon the beaten and bleeding form of His Son, hanging upon a Roman cross. Concerning His Son, He addressed the serpent, in Genesis 3:15:

> **Genesis 3:15.** I will put enmity between you and the woman, and between your seed and her seed; He shall strike your head, and you shall strike His heel. [Adapted from the ESV]

Recall that this is the first proclamation of the gospel, and it is therefore called the ***protoevangelium***. Thus, the motifs of The Seed of the Woman, The Acceptable Sacrifice, and The Gospel are tightly intertwined with that of The Invasion of Evil, Sin, and Death.

Q 17.   Think about just how the invasion of evil, sin, and death marred God's perfect creation. Discuss how you would respond to this assertion: the overarching theme of the Bible is good against evil.

Notes and Reflections

Session 4. The Invasion of Evil, Sin, and Death –
Part Two

Subsumed beneath The Invasion of Evil, Sin, and Death is a corollary motif: Divine Judgment and the Fear of Yahweh.

Noah's Flood

Intertwined with The Invasion of Evil, Sin, and Death motif is the sub-motif of The Divine Judgment and the Fear of Yahweh. In fact, these two motifs are so tightly coupled that they seem to blend into a single major biblical theme.

The first evidence of The Divine Judgment and the Fear of Yahweh motif is God's cataclysmic judgment of mankind recorded for us in the 6th through the 8th chapters of Genesis; namely, the Flood of Noah.

Reading through the first six chapters of Genesis, it is evident that the problem of evil, sin, and death had seriously mushroomed by the time we reach the 6th chapter.

Read Genesis 6.

Q 1. What specific condition caused God to bring the universal flood judgment to bear upon mankind? Why was a complete cleansing of the earth and its inhabitants necessary? Do you believe God's judgment was justified?

> *Genesis 6:5-6.* Yahweh saw that the wickedness of man was great in the earth, and that every intention of the thoughts of his heart was only evil continually. And

35

Yahweh was sorry that He had made man on the earth, and it grieved Him to his heart. [Adapted from the ESV]

Q 2. What glimmer of hope for mankind is provided by Genesis 6:8, and how was God's protection of Noah and his family related to the Seed of the Woman motif upon which we touched in Session 1?

Q 3. Can righteousness co-exist with evil?

We suggest that Yahweh Elohim brought about the universal Flood judgment to protect the seed of the woman from being corrupted by the great evil that was literally engulfing all of mankind. That seed was being passed through Noah to his son, Shem. Thus, nested within the Flood judgment is Yahweh's gracious deliverance of Noah, his family, and the animals He brought to the Ark to board it with Noah.

Read Matthew 24:36-44.

Q 4. What comparison does Jesus make between Noah's flood and His return? What is the significance of this comparison?

Jesus likens the judgment that will occur when He returns to that which occurred "in the days of Noah." At His second coming,

Christ will gather His elect into a place of protection while He banishes the rest of humanity into death.

Noah's Curse upon Canaan

Read Genesis 9:18-29.

Q 5. What occurred in this passage that caused Noah to place a curse on Canaan and how did it impact future generations?

In this episode, Noah became drunk from too much wine, and lay naked and uncovered in his tent. Evidently, his grandson, Canaan, came upon his grandfather lying naked in the tent, and reported this to his father, Ham, in a manner disrespectful of Noah. When Shem and Japheth heard of it, they covered their father with a garment while not allowing themselves to gaze upon his nakedness. Noah's curse is recorded in the following verses.

> **Genesis 6:24-27.** When Noah awoke from his wine and knew what his youngest son had done to him, he said, "Cursed be Canaan; a servant of servants shall he be to his brothers." He also said, "Blessed be Yahweh, the Elohim of Shem; and let Canaan be his servant. May God enlarge Japheth, and let him dwell in the tents of Shem, and let Canaan be his servant." [Adapted from the ESV]

Q 6. How did this curse play out during the times of the Conquest when Joshua was told to annihilate the Canaanites?

By means of this curse, Noah prophetically defined the theological, moral, and ethical trajectories of the people groups that would emanate from his three sons. In particular, he lays down the prophetic foundation for Shem's family to displace the descendants of Canaan from the Levant (the eastern Mediterranean region bounded on the north by the Euphrates River and on the south by the Sinai wilderness; the Levant encompasses modern Syria, Lebanon, Israel, and Jordan). This occurred centuries later during the Conquest recorded in the Book of Joshua.

The Tower of Babel

In our discussion of Motif #9 in Session 2, I pointed out that the Hebrew word which is customarily translated "Babel" in the 11th chapter of Genesis is identically the same as that translated "Babylon" at later points in the Hebrew Scriptures. The word is rendered correctly in the HCSB so as to clarify the linkage between the episode recorded in the 11th chapter of Genesis with the ancient city of Babylon, which was notorious in the ancient world for its idolatry and immorality. Throughout the Bible, Babylon is the paradigmatic City of Man that stands in relentless hostility against the Kingdom of God.

During the period of approximately five centuries that elapsed between the flood and the tower of Babel, the earth once again flourished.

Q 7. Did the universal Flood judgment inflicted by Yahweh Elohim cause man to change his moral and ethical behavior? Present the rationale for your answer from Scripture. What theological principle does this illustrate?

Read Genesis 1:28, Genesis 9:1-7, and Genesis 11:1-9.

Q 8. What specific command did the people disobey, and why was this a problem? What was God's intention regarding the distribution of human population across the earth?

After the Flood, the human population evidently mushroomed. Instead of scattering to fill the earth as Yahweh Elohim had commanded, a concentration of population developed somewhere in the Tigris-Euphrates basin – that is, the region which is now Iraq.

> **Genesis 11:1-9.** At one time the whole earth had the same language and vocabulary. As people migrated from the east, they found a valley in the land of Shinar and settled there. They said to each other, "Come, let us make oven-fired bricks." They used brick for stone and asphalt for mortar. And they said, "Come, let us build ourselves a city and a tower with its top in the sky. Let us make a name for ourselves; otherwise, we will be scattered over the face of the whole earth." Then Yahweh came down to look over the city and the tower that the men were building. Yahweh said, "If they have begun to do this as one people all having the same language, then nothing they plan to do will be impossible for them. Come, let Us go down there and confuse their language so that they will not understand one another's speech." So from there Yahweh scattered them over the face of the whole earth, and they stopped building the city. Therefore its name is called Babylon, for there Yahweh confused the language of the whole earth, and from there Yahweh scattered them over the face of the whole earth. [Adapted from the HCSB]

Q 9.   According to this passage, where did the people choose to live? What were some of the factors that played into their decision?

Not only did Yahweh confuse the language of mankind, thereby dividing humanity into multiple, distinct language and ethnic groups, but also He forced their dispersion according to Paul's statement:

> **Acts 17:26.**   And He made from one man every nation of mankind to live on all the face of the earth, having determined allotted periods and the boundaries of their dwelling place...   [Adapted from the ESV]

Figure 2 presents an artistic conception of the tower. It was probably constructed in the form of a ziggurat with a broad base and each successive layer indented until it reached a great height. The ziggurat was an artificial mountain that towered above the dust of the desert and the top of which touched the clouds.

2. The Tower of Babel

Q 10. Availing yourself of online resources, attempt to answer this question: what was the religious and theological significance of the Tower of Babel being in the form of a ziggurat?

Q11. What was God's ultimate purpose in the Tower of Babel incident?

Once again, as in the Flood episode, Yahweh acted to restrain human iniquity and sin in order to protect the Seed of the Woman from corruption. In addition, Yahweh's action amounts to a warning against large concentrations of human population in cities, for in such concentrations human iniquity and sin is intensified and multiplied.

Destruction of the Cities of the Plain

Sodom and its four associated cities were located in the plain that surrounds the point where the Jordan River enters the Dead Sea.

Read Genesis 19:1-29.

Q 12. Describe God's judgment upon Sodom and its associated cities. According to Scripture, what was the reason for this judgment?

The 19th chapter of Genesis records the second cataclysmic judgment – the destruction of Sodom, Gomorrah, and other nearby cities located in the fertile plain of the Jordan river just north of the Dead Sea. Since these were Canaanite cities, their destruction represents the first phase of Yahweh's judgment of the descendants of Canaan in light of Noah's curse, which we considered in the 9th chapter of Genesis.

Q 13. After having carefully read the narrative in the 19th chapter of Genesis, list the characters in the story. Analyze how the narrator characterizes each of these persons. Does later Scripture refer to Lot's wife?

Nested within this judgment episode is Yahweh's gracious deliverance of Lot and his two daughters. The Apostle Peter reflects on the evident display of the grace of Yahweh.

> **2 Peter 2: 5-9.** If He did not spare the ancient world, but preserved Noah, a herald of righteousness, with seven others, when He brought a flood upon the world of the ungodly; if by turning the cities of Sodom and Gomorrah to ashes He condemned them to extinction, making them an example of what is going to happen to the ungodly; and if he rescued righteous Lot, greatly distressed by the sensual conduct of the wicked (for as that righteous man lived among them day after day, he was tormenting his righteous soul over their lawless deeds that he saw and heard); then Yahweh knows how to rescue the godly from trials, and to keep the unrighteous under punishment until the day of judgment... [Adapted from the ESV]

Read Genesis 13:8-18.

Q 14. According to this passage, what was Lot's stated reason for moving to the Jordan valley? Why do you suppose he settled in one of the cities of the plain?

Q 15. Why does God allow cataclysmic judgments? What cataclysmic events have occurred in your lifetime, and how have they impacted you?

We believe all the great cataclysmic judgments that have occurred in history are intended by Yahweh to instill fear in the human heart, and to motivate men to walk in the way of Yahweh.

The Golden Calf Episode

Read Exodus 32.

Following the flow of Figure 1, the next passage that adds significantly to our understanding of The Invasion of Evil, Sin, and Death motif is the golden calf episode. While this is not the first passage in the Torah that mentions the sin of idolatry, it is the best passage on the subject in that it represents idolatry in all of its hideous detail.

Q 16. Describe the context of this passage. What is Moses doing while Aaron is forming the golden calf? Carefully analyze the theological significance of these contemporaneous activities.

How sad that during the very time Moses was on the summit of Mt. Sinai receiving instructions for the design and construction of the tabernacle, the people of Israel were in the valley below making this demand upon Aaron.

> **Exodus 32:1**. When the people saw that Moses delayed to come down from the mountain, the people gathered themselves together to Aaron and said to him, "Up, make us gods who shall go before us. As for this Moses, the man who brought us up out of the land of Egypt, we do not know what has become of him." [ESV]

The casting and forming of the golden calf were no small project, requiring considerable time and skill to complete.

Q 17. Compare and contrast the forming of the golden calf image with the construction of the tabernacle, which is described later in Exodus beginning with the 35th chapter. What is the theological significance of these two projects?

This example of idolatrous workmanship is placed in stark contrast to the God-ordained project of fabricating and constructing the tabernacle and all of its furnishings that is recorded in Exodus 35-39. Once the fabrication of the golden calf had been completed, and it had been set up, take careful note of how the people of Israel represented it.

> **Exodus 32:4.** These are your gods (= elohim), O Israel, who brought you up out of the land of Egypt! [ESV]

Compare this proclamation with Yahweh's statement concerning Himself in Exodus 20:2.

Q 18. What is your reaction to Aaron's actions and the people's proclamation above?

These people, who just a few short months earlier had experienced the Passover, had walked across the Red Sea on dry ground, and had experienced miraculous gifts of manna and water, now assigned to the golden calf the title, elohim, and attributed to it the action of delivering them from Egypt, which Yahweh Elohim had attributed to Himself in the prohibition against idolatry!

> **Exodus 20:2-6.** I am Yahweh your Elohim, who brought you out of the land of Egypt, out of the house of slavery. You shall have no other gods before me. You shall not make for yourself a carved image, or any likeness of anything that is in heaven above, or that is in the earth beneath, or that is in the water under the earth. You shall not bow down to them or serve them, for I, Yahweh your Elohim, am a jealous God, visiting the iniquity of the fathers on the children to the third and the fourth generation of those who hate me, but showing steadfast love to thousands of those who love me and keep my commandments. [Adapted from the ESV]

After the idolatrous proclamation of the people in Exodus 32:4, Aaron proclaimed a "festival to Yahweh" in the 5th verse. After idolatrous worship of the golden calf, this festival evidently devolved into a sexual orgy.

45

Q 19. Carefully analyze the golden calf episode and derive from it the cardinal elements of the sin of idolatry.

Take careful note of the parameters of idolatry as follows:

Construction of an object to take the place of Yahweh Elohim.

Representation of that object through language as having divine properties, including the ability to guide and direct human persons.

Worship of the object.

Engagement in revelry, including possibly a perverted sexual component.

These parameters are paradigmatic; that is, they define the actions that constitute and attend the sin of idolatry.

Q 20. Is idolatry limited to the worship of concrete material objects such as the golden calf? Discuss the rationale for your answer.

Read Ezekiel 14:1-8.

In our study of Book 3 on representations, we learned about godly and ungodly representational worlds. It is quite possible to fabricate an immaterial idol of the heart or mind.

Q 21. Identify and discuss a modern example against the parameters of idolatry listed above.

One prime example of an idol that is a mental construct is the infinite-time-plus-chance machine of Darwinian evolution.

Q 22. Examine the infinite-time-plus-chance machine of Darwinian evolution against the parameters of idolatry listed above. Analyze and discuss the ways in which it either does or does not correlate with these parameters.

Q 23. Analyze and discuss the ways in which the infinite-time-plus-chance machine of Darwinian evolution aids and abets human immorality of all forms.

The Divine Judgment and the Fear of Yahweh motif is one that we see played out in every era and society of human history. In particular, consider the 9/11 attacks on the twin towers in New York City. As in this instance, God's judgment may take the form of man-caused disasters. Even in the midst of this horrific event, in which thousands of people lost their lives, there were countless stories of God's intervention in miraculously protecting and rescuing others. He is always at work, exercising mercy and grace even in the context of judgment.

In other words, God's purpose in judgment always has a redemptive dimension. God uses natural disasters and other devastating events to place in evidence human wickedness and to showcase His glory. How do we respond when catastrophe strikes? Do we shake our fists toward heaven in prideful rebellion against Yahweh, or do we submit to Him and rest in His protection?

Notes and Reflections

Session 5. The Invasion of Evil, Sin, and Death – Part Three

Prophetic Passages on the Nature and Character of Sin

There are two passages in the prophetic literature of the Hebrew Scriptures which add to our understanding of the nature of sin: the 1st chapter of Isaiah and the 16th chapter of Ezekiel. Both employ figurative language to accurately represent the nature and character of sin.

Read Isaiah 1:1-23.

Q 1. List some examples of Judah's rebellious ways based upon this passage.

One observation you may have made is that the people were like rebellious children.   The Hebrew verb pasha translated "rebelled" means to rebel or transgress.

The people were rebellious, senseless, and sinful, and they caused physical harm to one another. The 4th verse is especially noteworthy in regard to the nature and character of sin:

Isaiah 1:4

Ah, sinful nation,
> a people laden with iniquity,
> offspring of evildoers,
> children who deal corruptly!
They have forsaken Yahweh,
They have despised the Holy One of Israel,

49

they are utterly estranged. [Adapted from the ESV]

The following list provides some insight into the meaning of important Hebrew words and how they are translated into the ESV.

3. Hebrew to English Word Translations

Hebrew Word	English Translation	Meaning
Chata	Sinful	To miss the mark of take a wrong path. This word is equivalent in meaning to the Greed *hamartia*.
Avon	Iniquity	Systematically evil, corrupt in nature.
Shacath	Deal corruptly	To go to ruin.
Raa	Evildoers	To be evil or bad.
Naats	Despised	To treat with contempt.
Zur	Estranged	To be a stranger.

Q 2.   Based upon Isaiah's language in the entire passage, Isaiah 1:1-23, what was the effect of Israel's sin on the moral and ethical health of the nation?

Q 3.   To what extent does Isaiah's indictment represent the moral and ethical climate in our world today?

Read Ezekiel 16:1-63.

This passage is an allegorical representation of the idolatry of Jerusalem as the spiritual equivalent of adultery.

Q 4. Identify as many allegorical components as you are able and identify who or what each component represents.

Q 5. List as many noteworthy observations as you are able to derive from this passage regarding the nature and character of Israel's sin against Yahweh?

Here the city of Jerusalem represents the entire nation of Israel. The theological framework for the allegory is that Yahweh Elohim has taken Israel unto Himself like a husband takes a wife. In addition, the covenant binding Israel to Yahweh is like the covenant of marriage. For Israel to break her covenant with Yahweh is like a wife who turns from her husband and goes after other lovers. So blatant is Israel's sin that she had become like a wanton prostitute!

Because of the hideousness of Israel's sin, Yahweh had no choice but to issue her a divorce certificate. While the word "divorce" does not occur in Ezekiel 16, the outpouring of the wrath of Yahweh is clearly and emphatically stated in Ezekiel 16:35ff. Moreover, divorce is explicitly stated in Isaiah 50:1 and Jeremiah 3:8. Thus, the marriage metaphor, as it applies to the relationship between Yahweh and Israel, was formally broken, but not without remedy.

Chata and Avon

These two Hebrew words, which surfaced in Isaiah's indictment of Judah and Jerusalem, deserve some additional comment. With respect to the sin of idolatry, Yahweh states the following in the 20th chapter of Exodus:

> **Exodus 20:5-6.** *You shall not bow down to them or serve them, for I, Yahweh your Elohim, am a jealous God, visiting the iniquity (= avon) of the fathers on the children to the third and the fourth generation of those who hate me, but showing steadfast love to thousands of those who love me and keep my commandments.*
> [Adapted from the ESV]

In seeming contradiction of this clear statement, Ezekiel addresses the issue of each generation being punished for its own sin in the 18th chapter of his prophecy as follows:

> **Ezekiel 18:20.** The soul who sins (= chata) shall die. The son shall not suffer for the iniquity (= avon) of the father, nor the father suffer for the iniquity (= avon) of the son. The righteousness of the righteous shall be upon himself, and the wickedness of the wicked shall be upon himself.

Q 6. How would you explain Exodus 20:5 vis-a-vis Ezekiel 18:20 in regard to the manner in which a generation is impacted by the moral failings of the preceding one?

I submit the key to the explanation lies in the use of the word "visiting" in Exodus 20:5. Keep in mind that chata designates a willful act of falling short or turning in a wrong direction, whereas avon means a systemic evil or corruption of nature.

The avon of the fathers is visited upon their children in the sense that a person's moral tendencies are genetically transmitted to the next generation, even as physical attributes are transmitted. It is in our DNA! Thus, a father who has a problem with alcoholism, sexual immorality, or other moral weakness should be alert to his children inheriting that same weakness. This is the meaning of Exodus 20:5.

Personal Responsibility

However, even in the face of the genetic transmission of avon, each person is responsible for his chata – that is, his willful acts of falling short or going astray from the right path. In other words, in spite of the fact that I may have inherited from my father a tendency toward alcoholism, for example, I am still responsible for self-discipline and moderation in the consumption of alcohol. In other words, I cannot shield myself from guilt before God on account of inherited avon, because I am personally responsible for my own chata. This is the meaning of Ezekiel 18:20 when read in the context of the entire chapter.

Q 7. How does understanding the difference between avon and chata help you counteract a victim mentality, as expressed by "the devil made me do it?"

Q 8. What can a father do to mitigate his children's or grandchildren's inherited sinful tendencies?

Read Leviticus 18:22-23, Leviticus 20:13-16, and Romans 1:26-27.

Q 9. How and to what extent do these passages bear upon the sexual orientation debate?

Q 10. Recall the definitions of chata and avon. How would you apply these terms to deviant sexual behavior?

The *chata* versus *avon* issue is especially relevant to the current debate over sexual orientation. The fact that homosexuality is an example of avon is indisputable based upon the explicit teaching of the above passages. However, the fact that a tendency toward homosexuality may be present in a person's DNA does not shield him from responsibility for righteous behavior in his own sexual interactions. Should he give way to his inherited tendency and practice homosexual intercourse, then this would be a *chata*, and in the words of Ezekiel, "The soul who sins *(= chata)* shall die."

The Death of Jesus Christ

What does the death of Jesus Christ, the Son of God, teach us concerning The Invasion of Evil, Sin, and Death?

> **Genesis 2:16-17.** And Yahweh Elohim commanded the man, "You are free to eat from any tree of the garden, but you must not eat from the tree of the knowledge of good

and evil, for on the day you eat from it, you will certainly die." [Adapted from the HCSB]

According to Genesis 2:17, the sin of eating of the forbidden fruit was a **capital offense** before God.

For us to regard sin as God does, we must learn to represent it as a treasonous act of prideful rebellion against the rule of God.

Q 11. What type of sin comes to mind when you think of capital punishment? What about small, seemingly insignificant sins?

James 2:10. For whoever keeps the whole law but fails in one point has become accountable for all of it. [From the ESV]

The fact that the entire human race is infected by evil, sin, and death requires a radical rescue and deliverance. Because of who Jesus Christ is – the Son of God and the Son of Man – His death places in evidence the magnitude of the problem of evil, sin, and death. If we perceive in the death of Jesus only a righteous man dying for the sins of others, we fail to see that death through the eyes of faith.

When Jesus died, He died as both the Son of Man and the Son of God! By virtue of His humanity, He was qualified to stand in our place and take our punishment upon Himself. By virtue of His deity, the magnitude or weight of His death was more than enough to satisfy the requirements of divine justice.

We can measure the magnitude or weight of the death of Christ by this: it was equivalent to the eternal death that each and every one of us would have to suffer, had He not died in our place.

The death of Christ was equivalent to the sum total of the eternal deaths that the entire human population of the world for all time would have to suffer in order to make up to God an adequate apology and satisfaction for the capital offense of human sin. This is HUGE!

Q 12. What is your reaction to the extent and significance to Christ's death?

The Teaching of the Apostle Paul

The Apostle Paul certainly had much to say about the problem of evil, sin, and death.

Read Romans 7 in its context.

Q 13. What struggle does Paul deal with in this chapter? Have you ever experienced a similar struggle?

While there is intense debate over the precise interpretation of this chapter, let us back off and consider the overall trajectory of Paul's argument. Importing his terminology from Romans 8:2, he asserts that there is present in the human personality a law of sin and death. In Romans 7:7ff, he represents this law of sin and death as if it were an active agent in the human personality that responds in a pernicious way to the righteous requirements of God as expressed in His moral law.

Q 14. How does the law of sin and death respond to the commandments of God?

According to the Apostle Paul, the law of sin and death that permeates our members – especially or brains – responds to God's commandments by causing an impulse toward disobedience rather than one toward obedience. In other words, the law of sin and death is another name for the pernicious kernel of prideful rebellion that lurks in the human heart. To use Paul's example in Romans 7:7, the prideful rebellion of the human heart responds to the commandment, "You shall not covet," by energizing all manner of covetousness. The same could be said concerning each of the commandments.

Q 15. Returning to the golden calf episode, analyze how the people of Israel responded to the commandment, "You shall have no other gods before Me," in the context of Paul's teaching in the 7th chapter of Romans.

The Teaching of James

There is one more passage we must consider before concluding this discussion of The Invasion of Evil, Sin, and Death.

Read James 1:12-18.

Q 16. What is the focus of James' teaching in this passage as it applies to The Invasion of Evil, Sin, and Death motif?

In essence, James teaches us that all temptations – that is, solicitations toward evil – spring from the human heart. We have only ourselves to blame, not the Devil, and certainly not God. The strategy for conquering temptation is, first, to recognize it in its germinal form; that is, when it is just beginning to sprout. Instead of mentally watering and nurturing it, we must ruthlessly pull it up like a noxious weed and put it in the trash!

While our discussion of this motif seems lengthy, we have only touched the surface. Many other passages of Scripture inform and illuminate the significance of the problem of evil, sin, and death. For example, Jesus' teaching in the Sermon on the Mount represents sin not only in terms of external behavior but also as internal thoughts and lusts. As you read through Scripture from year to year, you can add your own insights to this discussion.

Think back on the judgments we have discussed and list the evidence of God's love and grace even in the context of judgment. Think also of His protection of the seed of the woman in preserving the ancestral line of Jesus Christ from being eradicated.

Although this motif may appear to some people as dark and discouraging, always keep in mind God's character – that He is a loving, holy God, and therefore cannot tolerate sin. Sin must be judged, but in that judgment God reveals love, grace, mercy, and patience. His goal is always repentance, but His patience will eventually give way to judgment, as it did with the nation of Israel during the time of Jeremiah and the Babylonian conquest of Judah and Jerusalem.

Notes and Reflections

Session 6. The Temple

The Temple is Motif #2, upon which we briefly touched in Session 1. This motif is special and precious in that it represents the holiness of God and how we, as sinful people, may approach and worship Him. Since a temple is a special place or sphere in which man can worship and enjoy fellowship with God, it follows that a temple doesn't necessarily require a building. However, at the proper time Yahweh did deliver instructions to Moses to build a unique place of worship known as the Tabernacle, upon which we touched in Session 5 of SG3. This was the forerunner of Solomon's Temple, one of the most magnificent structures in the ancient world.

The Temple motif is highly symbolic, with object lessons abounding, including in its design, in its furnishings, and in the associated Levitical system of worship. Perhaps the greatest symbolism is the manner in which these aspects of The Temple point to the Lord Jesus Christ as the "Lamb of God who takes away the sin of the world," in the words of John the Baptist as recorded in John 1:29. Indeed, there are profound theological truths that are objectified, and thereby clarified, by the imagery of The Temple as revealed in Scripture.

Introduction in the Torah

As we reflect on The Temple motif, Solomon's Temple (ca. 10th through 6th century BC) or the Herodian Temple (ca. 1st century AD) may come to mind. Or, our thoughts may take us back to the book of Exodus beginning in the 25th chapter where Moses received instructions from Yahweh for constructing the Tabernacle in the wilderness. But is that the first mention of a place of worship in the biblical record? Consider the following verse.

> **Genesis 3:8.** And they heard the sound of Yahweh Elohim walking in the garden in the cool of the day, and the man and his wife hid themselves from the presence of the Yahweh Elohim among the trees of the garden. [Adapted from the ESV]

Q 1. According to this verse, where was the first temple?

Does it surprise you to learn that the garden of Eden was God's original temple on earth – the place where He chose to fellowship with man face to face? God's plan included worship and fellowship from the very time of man's creation!

Q 2. Take a few moments to reflect on this insight. How often have your praise and adoration of Yahweh been spurred by seeing a beautiful sunset or towering mountain. We see God in His creation – and that elicits our worship and praise.

Adam was given the role of the primordial temple caretaker, much like the ancient Levitical priests of Moses' time.

Think back to the previous motif we studied, that of The Invasion of Evil, Sin, and Death.

Q 3. What event occurred that destroyed temple worship for Adam and Eve?

This incident, which we know as the Fall, changed the course of history for all mankind, and resulted in the expulsion of man from the Garden Temple.

> **Genesis 3:24.** He (God) drove out the man, and at the east of the garden of Eden He placed the cherubim and a

flaming sword that turned every way to guard the way to the tree of life.

In effect, the temple moved from the interior of the garden of Eden to its eastern entrance, and man was barred from entering the garden.

The Genesis narrative records numerous episodes in which the patriarchs built altars and worshipped Yahweh at places which were special to them. An important example is Bethel where Jacob spent the night when he was fleeing to escape the wrath of his brother Esau as recorded in the 28th chapter of Genesis. In fact, the name of this special place means "house of God."

Development in the Hebrew Scriptures

Scan Exodus 25-31.

This extended passage records Yahweh's detailed specifications for the Tabernacle in the wilderness, a portable worship center. By means of the Tabernacle and the Levitical worship conducted therein, fallen man could once again approach and enjoy fellowship with Yahweh, the absolutely holy God of Israel. The layout of the Tabernacle is delineated in Figure 3.

4. Layout of the Tabernacle in the Wilderness

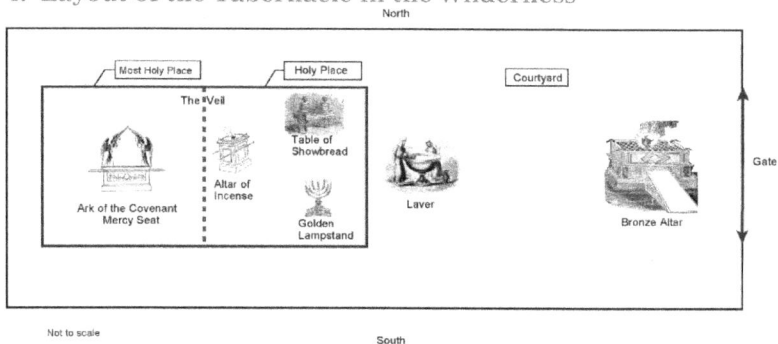

North

Most Holy Place | Holy Place | Courtyard

The Veil

Table of Showbread

Ark of the Covenant Mercy Seat | Altar of Incense | Golden Lampstand | Laver | Bronze Altar

Gate

Not to scale

South

Q 4. Compare and contrast the interaction between God and man that took place in the primordial Garden Temple with that which occurred in the Tabernacle in the wilderness. Identify and list ways in which the Tabernacle represents God's love and grace toward mankind?

5. Seeing Jesus in the Tabernacle

Q 5. For each illustration below, attempt to relate each of the components of the Tabernacle with the life and ministry of Jesus Christ. For each Tabernacle component include at least one reference to the Christian Scriptures that supports your proposed relationship. I have filled in the information for the Courtyard Entrance and the Courtyard as examples.

Courtyard Entrance
The courtyard had a single entrance, even as Jesus Christ is the only way to God (John 14:6).

The courtyard marked the boundary between the holy
and the common, and only the Aaronic priests could
move freely within the courtyard. Jesus sanctified
Himself that He might, in turn, sanctify those the Father
has given Him. (John 17:17-19, Hebrews 9:13-14, and
Hebrews 13:12-13.

8 The Laver

9 The Table of Showbread

10 The Altar of Incense

11 The Golden Lampstand

12 The Veil

13 The Ark of the Covenant and Mercy Seat

The Book of Hebrews contains rich teaching concerning the manner in which the Tabernacle and associated worship rituals represent the redemptive ministry of Jesus Christ. The following five passages are noteworthy examples.

67

Hebrews 4:14-16. Since then we have a great high priest who has passed through the heavens, Jesus, the Son of God, let us hold fast our confession. For we do not have a high priest who is unable to sympathize with our weaknesses, but one who in every respect has been tempted as we are, yet without sin. Let us then with confidence draw near to the throne of grace, that we may receive mercy and find grace to help in time of need. [ESV]

Hebrews 5:1-10. For every high priest chosen from among men is appointed to act on behalf of men in relation to God, to offer gifts and sacrifices for sins. He can deal gently with the ignorant and wayward, since he himself is beset with weakness. Because of this he is obligated to offer sacrifice for his own sins just as he does for those of the people. And no one takes this honor for himself, but only when called by God, just as Aaron was. So also Christ did not exalt himself to be made a high priest, but was appointed by him who said to him, "You are my Son, today I have begotten you;" as he says also in another place, "You are a priest forever, after the order of Melchizedek." In the days of his flesh, Jesus offered up prayers and supplications, with loud cries and tears, to him who was able to save him from death, and he was heard because of his reverence. Although he was a son, he learned obedience through what he suffered. And being made perfect, he became the source of eternal salvation to all who obey him, being designated by God a high priest after the order of Melchizedek. [ESV]

Hebrews 6:17-20. So when God desired to show more convincingly to the heirs of the promise the unchangeable character of his purpose, he guaranteed it with an oath, so that by two unchangeable things, in which it is impossible for God to lie, we who have fled for refuge might have strong encouragement to hold fast to the hope set before us. We have this as a sure and steadfast anchor of the soul, a hope that enters into the Most Holy Place behind the curtain, where Jesus has gone as a forerunner on our behalf, having become a high priest forever after the order of Melchizedek. [Adapted from the ESV]

Hebrews 9:1-7. Now even the first covenant had regulations for worship and an earthly place of holiness. For a tent was prepared, the first section, in which were the lampstand and the table and the bread of the Presence. It is called the Holy Place. Behind the second curtain was a second section called the Most Holy Place, having the golden altar of incense and the ark of the covenant covered on all sides with gold, in which was a golden urn holding the manna, and Aaron's staff that budded, and the tablets of the covenant. Above it were the cherubim of glory overshadowing the mercy seat. Of these things we cannot now speak in detail. These preparations having thus been made, the priests go regularly into the first section, performing their ritual duties, but into the second only the high priest goes, and he but once a year, and not without taking blood, which he offers for himself and for the unintentional sins of the people. [ESV]

Hebrews 10:19-22. Therefore, brothers, since we have confidence to enter the Most Holy Place by the blood of Jesus, by the new and living way that he opened for us through the curtain, that is, through his flesh, and since we have a great priest over the house of God, let us draw near with a true heart in full assurance of faith, with our hearts sprinkled clean from an evil conscience and our bodies washed with pure water. [Adapted from the ESV]

Q 6. Using insights gleaned from these five passages, together with any other passages from Hebrews that you have studied, augment your answer to the previous question in regard to the representational significance of the Tabernacle components and associated worship rituals.

Q 7. Imagine yourself being conducted on a tour of the Tabernacle by Jesus Christ Himself, our Great High Priest. Formulate a narrative of what would He say to you as you pause to consider each feature of the Tabernacle and its furnishings: the brazen altar of sacrifice; the laver; in the Holy Place, the table of showbread on your right, the golden altar of incense directly in front of you, and the lampstand on your left; finally, as He draws back the massive curtain, you enter the Most Holy Place with the Ark of Covenant, the over-shadowing cherubim, and the Shekinah Glory. Describe your heart's response as you ponder the significance of each of these features.

Eventually the portable tabernacle was replaced by the magnificent temple in Jerusalem built by King Solomon in the 10th century BC. The Solomonic temple is designated the First Temple, and it was destroyed by the Babylonians in the early 6th century BC. Some 70 years later, under the authority of Cyrus, the Jews were allowed to return to Jerusalem and to rebuild the temple on its site; this temple is designated the Second Temple. It was improved and expanded in stages until the time of Herod the Great, who authorized the building of the magnificent Herodian Temple, which is where Jesus worshiped and taught. It was destroyed by the Roman legions under the command of Titus in 70 AD.

Fulfillment

Read Hebrews 10.

This passage reveals the fact that the tabernacle and temple of the Hebrew Scriptures were actually a shadow and prefigurement of something much more significant, which was enacted in the life, death, burial and resurrection of Jesus Christ.

Q 8.   Summarize how this chapter from Hebrews enhances your understanding of the priestly ministry of Jesus Christ. Select one passage from this chapter, memorize it, and then share it with your fellow students as you participate in the group discussion of this session.

John 2:19. Jesus answered them, "Destroy this temple, and in three days I will raise it up." [ESV]

Q 9.   Considering the context of this verse, what is its meaning and its application within the framework of The Temple motif?

Read Ephesians 2:19-22 and 1 Peter 2:4-10.

Q 10. According to these Scriptures, where is the temple of God today? Discuss the implications of your answer based on our careful study of the Tabernacle and its representational significance.

Culmination

We have traced The Temple motif from Genesis through the entire Bible and have now come to the final book and the end of history.

Revelation 21:3-4. And I heard a loud voice from the throne saying, "Behold, the dwelling place of God is with man. He will dwell with them, and they will be His people, and God Himself will be with them as their God. [Adapted from the ESV]

Q 11. What is the location of the temple of God according to this passage? Discuss how God's original intent regarding His temple is consummated in His eternal kingdom.

This motif is so beautiful because it demonstrates that God's supreme desire and intent through all of human history is to dwell with us, and for us to dwell with Him. This was why we were created, and this is what we enjoyed in the Garden Temple. With the Fall came the breaking of this intimacy, and the rest of history is the story of God's relentless redemptive work to realize His original plan and purpose for mankind.

Q 12. Summarize the insights you have derived from the study of The Temple motif concerning the nature and character of God, how He relates to us, and how we are to worship Him.

Q 13. How does the insight that our bodies are now the temple of the living God impact your life and ministry in the present?

Q 14.   From your study of The Temple motif, what is the most important thing you have learned about the true nature of worship?

Notes and Reflections

Session 7. Review & Discussion

Just as we enjoy tracing various themes in a mystery novel, so we should develop an appreciation for the themes God has woven throughout the Bible. All major Bible themes have their inception in Torah, the first five books of the Bible. All fourteen of the integrative motifs are listed in Table 1, together with relevant Scripture passages.

Together we traced two integrative motifs, The Invasion of Evil, Sin, and Death and The Temple, as they were introduced in Torah, developed in the Hebrew Scriptures, passed through the Christ Event, and were culminated in the Christian Scriptures.

We discovered the significance of the Christ Event on both motifs was substantial. In the case of The Invasion of Evil, Sin, and Death motif, Christ defeated Satan once for all through His death. Moreover, He will bring about the ultimate destruction of Satan, as well as evil, sin, and death. The culmination, then, occurs in the New Jerusalem when Christ's victory is actualized. In the meantime, we regard Satan as a defeated foe!

In the Temple Motif, we came full circle as we considered God's primordial Garden Temple where He walked and talked in close relationship with Adam and Eve, through its development in the Hebrew Scriptures with the building of the Tabernacle and later the First and Second Temples. In the course of our discussion, we noted with great joy how each element of the tabernacle / temple pointed us to the redemptive ministry of Jesus Christ. The Christ Event was poignant in that at the very moment Christ gave up His spirit, the veil of the temple was torn in two from the top to the bottom, thereby manifesting the open access that Jesus had secured for us into the very presence of God. As we continued our discussion, we discovered that the Herodian Temple, destroyed by the Romans in 70 AD, has been replaced by the hearts of people like us who have become true followers of Jesus Christ. Our bodies are now the temple of the living God! And the glorious culmination of this theme is in Revelation 21:22, which states the following:

Revelation 21:22. And I saw no temple in the city, for its temple is the Lord God the Almighty and the Lamb. [ESV]

Motif	Scriptures
1. The Name of God	Gen 1:1; Gen 14:19-20; Gen 15:2; Gen 17:1; Exo 3:14; Joh 8:58; Acts 2:36
2. The Temple	Gen 1:26-28; Gen 2:15; Gen 3:8,24; Exo 25-31; 1 Ki 7,8; Joh 2:19; Heb 10; 1 Pet 2:4-10; Rev 21:3-4
3. The Sabbath	Gen 2:3; Exo 20:8; Exo 31:12; Lev 26; 2 Chr 36:17-27; Neh 9-10, 13; Isa 1; Isa 56; Isa 58:13-14; Mat 12:1-12; Mar 2:27-28; Heb 4
4. The Imago Deo (Man created in God's Image).	Gen 1:26-28, 2:7; Rom 8:29; 1 Cor 11:7; Col 1:15
5. The Marriage Metaphor	Gen 2:18-25; Mal 2:14; Mat 19:6; Eph 5:22-33; Rev 19:7
6. The Invasion of Evil, Sin, and Death	Gen 3:21; Gen 4; Lev 1-7; Heb 9:22; Lev 1:1-17; Rom 12:1-2
7. The Seed of the Woman	Genesis 3:1; Genesis 15:5; Romans 4; Galatians 3:16
8. The Acceptable Sacrifice	Gen 3:21; Gen 4; Lev 1:1-17; Lev 1-7; Heb 9:22; Rom 12:1-2
9. The city of Man vs. the Kingdom of God	Gen 11; Mat 5-7; Rev 17
10. The People of the New Way	Gen 12 & 15; Gen 18:19; Jos 24:15; Jdg 17:6; Jdg 21:25; Rom 11; Heb 11
11. The Gospel	Gen 3:15; Mat 28:18-20; John 3:1-17; Acts 3:25; Gal 3:8-9; 1 Cor 15:1-8; Col 2:13-15; Tit 2:11-14; Heb 2:14
12. Sovereign Election (SE) and Human Responsibility (HR)	SE: Rom 9:13; 2 Tim 2:19; Rom 8:29-30; Rom 9:19-24; Phil 2:12-13; 1 Pet 1:5. HR: Gen 2:17; Eph 1:11; Phi 2:12-13; Heb 11:39-12:2
13. The Prototype	Exo 1-17; 1 Cor 10:1-13; Heb 3:7-4; Heb 13

14. Covenant of Conditional Blessing	Exo 15:25-26; Deu 28-30; 2 Chr 7:14; 2 Ki 25:3; Neh 8-9

Discussion Questions

Q 1. Select at least two motifs and trace them through the Bible from their introduction in the Torah, through their development in the Hebrew Scriptures, through the Christ event, and to their consummation. You may use the information in Figure 5 as a point of departure for your study.

Q 2. Carefully examine and reflect upon the fourteen motifs and suggest ways in which they might be collected into logical groupings. A number of the motifs undergo a significant transformation as they pass through the Christ Event. Can you identify any that do not? Explain your answer.

Q 3. After exploring the Torah, suggest other integrative motifs that are not included among the fourteen listed in Table 1.

Q 4. How does understanding the flow of the integrative motifs enhance your understanding of God, His purposes, and His word?

ı

Q 5. Each of the motifs is like a strand in a tapestry. All are necessary and when blended together, create an object of beauty. Discuss how the strands of these motifs blend together to create a beautiful whole.

Q 6. Discuss the ways in which your studies in Book 5 has enhanced your understanding of the nature and character of God and your ability to worship Him in spirit and truth in accordance with John 4:24.

I encourage you to refer to chapter 5 in TR1 for development of other motifs.

Congratulations on completing Book 5. You are now ready to move to Book 6, The Two-Part Christian Gospel.

Notes and Reflections

Afterword

About Us

WitW is a product of Daystar Institute of Biblical Theology and Leadership Development (DI), which is dedicated to supporting local churches in fulfillment of their mission of making disciples of all nations. We have two offices: DI / NM is based in Albuquerque, New Mexico, and DI / A is based in Kampala, Uganda. Please do not hesitate to contact us at www.DaystarInstitute/NM.us if you have any questions or comments or wish to request training in the use of our materials.

Peter Briggs is founder and president-emeritus of Daystar Institute of Biblical Theology & Leadership Development. In addition to teaching and mentoring, Dr. Briggs has authored the WitW Study Guide Series to challenge students in uncompromising discipleship, practical Christian theology, and building a biblical worldview. The WitW study has had a great impact in both East Africa and the USA and is an excellent tool for encouraging and equipping disciples of Jesus to actually live out their faith.

Dedication

The *Walking in the Way of Christ & the Apostles Study Guide Series* is dedicated to Reverend Morris Wanje, whose prayers for God to raise up a means for strengthening and equipping young pastors and church leaders in East Africa caused the Holy Spirit of God to move upon the hearts of godly men and women at Daystar Institute/NM to create this study.

Acknowledgments

I am grateful for the heroic efforts of our team of contributors, editors, board of directors, and all who have had a part in the development of the WitW study. In particular, I extend my heartfelt gratitude to my wife, Rosemarie, our daughter, Ruthanne Hamrick, and ministry associates John & Marcie Kinzer, Stephen Patterson, and Michael & Antoninah Mutinda, for their valuable input and help with the Study Guide Series; and to Darienne Dumas and Emily Fuller for proof-reading the texts.

Testimonials

"The *Walking in the Way of Christ & the Apostles* (WitW) series by Dr. Peter Briggs is a powerful tool for fulfilling Jesus' universal mandate to make disciples. WitW is theologically sound, conceptually brilliant, and life- changing for those who are trained by it. The impact of WitW is not only personal transformation into the image of Christ, but also a profound influence on families, churches, and the larger culture, whether in America or Africa or anywhere else. Peter Briggs is a theologian of substantial import, but he has not merely plied his theological craft in the halls of academia. With God's enablement, he has managed to translate biblical truth and disciple-making principles into something that actually works in the real world! Those who embrace and employ *Walking in the Way* in their own lives will find themselves part of a movement affecting generations to come."

Steven Collins, PhD, Executive Dean, Trinity Southwest University

"*Walking in the Way of Christ & the Apostles* (WitW) is a magnificent literary work in biblical theology that offers the student an education in practical Christianity. The WitW study was first introduced in

November 2011; since that time we have been using it to instruct ministry leaders and rural pastors at a low cost, and the transformation of lives is phenomenal. Learners get to understand the message of the Bible and are able to study it effectively. In my own interaction with the material since 2012, I have come to realize that Jesus Christ is using it to revive His remnant in Kenya and other parts of Africa, teaching us how to think in a biblical way and be successful in all spheres of life. I am convinced that the WitW material holds the key to Africa's revival, and, in Yahweh's hand, it is a mighty tool for returning the continent back to Him."

Michael Mutinda, Team Leader, Daystar Institute / Africa

Walking in the Way of Christ & the Apostles
Study Guide Series

Part 1: Foundational Principles. These principles are foundational to equip the Christ-follower to have and to be governed by the mind of Christ.

1. The Way of God
2. The Storyline of the Bible
3. Biblical Reality
4. Discovering the Meaning of Scripture
5. Torah: The Fountainhead of Wisdom
6. The Two-Part Christian Gospel

Part 2: The Gospel of the Kingdom of God. Here we explore the ways in which the Christian gospel confronts the prideful rebellion of the human heart and exalts Christ as King over all.

7. Authority of the King
8. Called by the King
9. The Meaning of Discipleship
10. Disciplines of the Kingdom
11. Household of the King
12. The Second Coming of the King

Part 3 – The Gospel of God. This final set explores how the Christian gospel affords a complete solution to human depravity and the threefold problem of sin and death.

13. Introduction to the Gospel of God
14. The Reason for the Gospel of God
15. Content of the Gospel of God
16. Perversions of the Gospel of God
17. Application of the Gospel of God

Theological Readers (TR)

TR1 – Part 1: Foundational Principles
TR2 – Part 2: The Gospel of the Kingdom of God
TR3 – Part 3: The Gospel of God
TR4 – Resources and Appendices

Theological Handbooks (TH)

TH1 – Part 1: The Way of God
TH2 – Part 2
TH3 – Part 3

Connect with us at www.DaystarInstituteNM.us, or
Contact us via email at WalkingintheWayUSA@gmail.com

www.ingramcontent.com/pod-product-compliance
Lightning Source LLC
Chambersburg PA
CBHW071907020426
42331CB00010B/2710